BRISTOL CHANNEL SHIPPING MEMORIES

by
Andrew Wiltshire

The motor ore carrier *Afghanistan* of 1957 and her near sistership *Daghestan* of 1960 were regular callers at Cardiff and Newport with iron ore for nearby East Moors or Llanwern steelworks. They were owned by the Hindustan Steam Shipping Company which was a subsidiary of Common Brothers (Management). Having discharged at the iron ore berth in the Roath Dock, the *Afghanistan* sails from Cardiff on the evening high tide of 14 May 1972. Strangely her exhaust is emitting smoke rings. She ended her days in 1986 being scrapped in Spain.

INTRODUCTION

Geographically located on the West Coast of Great Britain the Bristol Channel has been a centre for sea born trade for many centuries. It does however have one of the largest tidal ranges in the world which brings with it a range of problems. Most ports consist of an enclosed dock system with access via locks. Restricted tidal access and small locks are two drawbacks with these enclosed dock systems. Tidal action and close proximity of river mouths ensure that regular dredging of approach channels is essential to prevent silting up.

The Bristol Channel has a number of ports on its northern shoreline which we recognise as the South Wales ports. These consist of Swansea, Port Talbot, Barry, Cardiff and Newport. All are currently trading in 2006 to varying extents. Further up the Bristol Channel on the southern shore things have changed somewhat over the last thirty years or so. At the mouth of the River Avon we have Avonmouth, still trading today. Portishead close by to the west has however closed to commercial traffic as has Bristol City Docks situated further up the River Avon. A new purpose-built dock was constructed close to Portishead and was christened Royal Portbury. Opened in 1977, it is capable of accommodating much larger vessels, and is a thriving port today.

This book looks at the period from the late 1960s to the early 1970s. This was when I first came into contact with the great variety of shipping to be seen visiting the various ports. It was also a time of change in Bristol Channel for a number of reasons. The roles of the ports themselves were being forced to change. The South Wales ports had for many years been thriving coal exporting centres but this was rapidly coming to an end. In fact by 1966 only Barry and Swansea were still active in this role. The coal handling facilities at Cardiff and Newport had been cleared away and the land allocated for new trades. The dock at Penarth had closed altogether and had been largely filled in. Trade at Avonmouth suffered less of an impact from these changes at this time, but would suffer in later years.

Ships too were changing. There were still many steam powered ships to be found calling in the Bristol Channel, but their numbers were dwindling by 1972. By then they were mostly sailing under flags of convenience. Ship design was subject to huge changes by the late 1960s. Conventional cargo ships, which had for so long been a feature in British Merchant fleets, were giving way to bulk carriers and container ships. Bristol Channel ports were not particularly suited to the newly established container trade growing in western Europe. Ports such as Felixstowe and Southampton, located closer to mainland Europe, were to benefit from containerisation.

<u>Acknowledgements</u>

A little while ago I came to the conclusion it was time to put a book together using some of my father's collection of shipping photographs, taken in the days when ships were plentiful and the sun always seemed to shine. John Wiltshire took a wealth of material in the Bristol Channel between 1967 and 1990. With his blessing I set about making a selection of some of the better shots in his collection, no easy task. All photographs in this book were taken by John Wiltshire unless stated otherwise. A thank you goes out to Derek Chaplin, Bob Allen and Nigel Jones who were also more than happy to let me feature some of their work.

A very big thank you must go to my good friend Kevin Blair and also to Paul Hood who have both helped enormously by providing facts and figures for some of the ships featured in this book. They have also tried where possible to enlighten us as to their fate. Many thanks also to Bernard McCall for his help and guidance, and to Gilbert Mayes for his usual thorough checking of the manuscript. Written sources used throughout include various volumes of *Lloyd's Register of Shipping*, old editions of *Ocean Ships*, *Cory Towage* (by W J Harvey) and *Blow Five* (by W B Hallam). Finally, I must thank Amadeus Press for their marvellous work in bringing the book to such a splendid conclusion.

Andrew Wiltshire   Cardiff   June 2006

Published by Bernard McCall, 400 Nore Road, Portishead, Bristol, BS20 8EZ, England. Website : www.coastalshipping.co.uk
Telephone/fax : 01275 846178. E-mail : bernard@coastalshipping.co.uk
All distribution enquiries should be addressed to the publisher.

Printed by Amadeus Press, Ezra House, West 26 Business Park, Cleckheaton, West Yorkshire, BD19 4TQ
Telephone : 01274 863210; fax : 01274 863211; e-mail : info@amadeuspress.co.uk; website : www.amadeuspress.co.uk

ISBN : 1-902953-25-8

Front cover : After picking up a pilot in Barry Roads the passenger/cargo vessel **City of Birmingham** of Ellerman Lines would continue her passage up to Avonmouth on the flood tide. She is seen on the final approach having just picked up the tugs that will take her into the lock. The date is 29 September 1968. *City of Birmingham* was registered in Glasgow and dates from 1949. Completed by John Browns of Clydebank, she had steam turbine propulsion. Her three turbines geared to a single shaft gave her a speed of 15.5 knots. She was scrapped in Spain in 1971.

Back cover : A Blue Star by night! The **Rockhampton Star** makes a fine sight as she lies on the Empire Cold Stores Wharf on 30 March 1971. Her funnel colours alone when illuminated are quite spectacular. The **Rockhampton Star** was built by Cammell Laird, c⸍ Birkenhead, in 1957 as a refrigerated cargo vessel for Blue Star Line. In her lifetime under the British flag she visited Cardiff on a number of occasions. She had a black hull when built but ended her days with a light grey hull. She was sold in 1981 for a further two years trading, ending her days with breakers in Bangladesh.

We begin our voyage of nostalgia in Swansea and we shall travel eastwards. T & J Harrison was a well known Liverpool-based general cargo shipping line. Their vessels traded to such places East and South Africa, Venezuela, Columbia and the West Indies. Harrison Line ships were a common sight in the Bristol Channel calling at Swansea, Cardiff and Avonmouth in particular. The motor ship *Wanderer* of 1951 was the third vessel in the fleet to carry that name, and is sailing light from Swansea in the evening sunshine of 28 June 1969. She may well have been moving to another UK port to load. In the background the stern tug *Alexandra* has just cast off while on the adjacent pier the tugs *Cambrian* and *Formby* await their next call of duty. The *Wanderer* was sold to Cypriot interests in 1972 and became the *Cleopatra*. As the Panamanian *Chung Thai*, she suffered a major engine breakdown on 17 July 1974, en route to Japan from Korea. She was subsequently sold for scrap to South Korean breakers at Masan two months later.

The motor coaster *Frederick T Everard* was built at Goole in 1954 for F T Everard & Sons. She had a gross tonnage of 2488 and was powered by a 6-cylinder Newbury diesel of 1600bhp. Here we see her manoeuvring in the Kings Dock on 4 September 1969. In the background are cargo ships of the Blue Funnel Line and Houlder Bros with the Maltese Cross on the funnel. Everards sold the *Frederick T Everard* in 1972 to Greek owners who named her *Emilia G*. After several changes of name she was broken up in 1982.

The **British Resource** was a fine example of a class of twenty similar motor tankers, delivered between 1948 and 1955, in the British Tanker Co (BP) fleet. They were approximately 16800 tonnes deadweight and were basically an enlarged version of a slightly earlier post-war design. **British Resource** was built in 1949 by Hawthorn Leslie at Newcastle upon Tyne and had a 6-cylinder Doxford oil engine. She could be found trading around the UK coast and northern Europe with refined products such as gasoline and diesel. She is seen sailing in dramatic autumn lighting conditions on 20 November 1970. The **British Resource** was to trade for a further seventeen months until her sale to Spanish breakers. She arrived at Castellon on 24 April 1972 and breaking up commenced the following month. BP adopted the colour scheme shown in the late 1960s with a simplified funnel colour and a move from a dark grey to a black hull.

A pair of Greek flag motor tankers in dry-dock and under repair on 29 September 1972. The drydock facilities at Swansea could handle quite large vessels and were often busy with a lot of work being carried out on tankers. The *Ionic Queen* of 1956 was built in the Netherlands as *Koningswaard*. The *Tavros* of 1955 was built at La Ciotat in southern France as *Biblos* for French owners.

The Royal Fleet Auxiliary tanker *Wave Baron* is seen here on the repair berth in the Queens Dock on 6 June 1969. She was launched by Furness Shipbuilding in 1946 as the *Empire Flodden* for the Admiralty. Her working career was nearly over in this view, as she went on to lay up at Devonport, before being sold for breaking up in Bilbao in 1972. The Queens Dock was the last dock to be built and opened in 1920. It was primarily an oil dock for tankers and was created by reclaiming land. It was built to serve BP's nearby Llandarcy oil refinery.

Swansea was always a good place to see one of Alfred Holt's distinctive Blue Funnel cargo liners. Blue Funnel traded principally between Europe and the Far East, mainly China, Japan and Indonesia. The *Demodocus* seen here on 4 September 1969, was a motor ship built in 1955 by Vickers Armstrong at Newcastle upon Tyne. She was powered by a 6-cylinder Harland & Wolff oil engine which gave her a speed of 15 knots. She could accommodate up to 18 passengers. Most ships in the Blue Funnel fleet at this time displayed common design characteristics. *Demodocus* was transferred to associated company Glen Line in 1970 and renamed *Glenroy*. She reverted to the name *Demodocus* and Blue Funnel colours in 1972, but was sold the following year to Nan Yang Shipping in Macao. She was renamed *Hungsia* until sold to China in 1979. The end came in 1982 when she was scrapped.

The Alexandra Towing Company became the sole tug operator at Swansea following the takeover of the Britannia Steam Towing fleet in 1962. There were still a number of steam tugs active in the early 1970s. The *Formby* of 1951 was previously a member of the Liverpool fleet and stayed at Swansea until 1969 when an Italian company bought her for further use at Brindisi, and named her *Poderoso*. She is thought to have been scrapped by 1998. The *Flying Kestrel* of 1943 was originally a Birch-class Empire tug named *Empire Mascot*. When purchased by Alexandra Towing in 1948, she was allocated to Southampton and moved to Swansea in the 1960s. She was sold to ship-breakers at Passage West near Cork in March 1969. The pair are seen close to the drydock entrance on 19 July 1968 as they leave the berth in tandem.

Dredging at South Wales ports was the responsibility of the Port Authority. Before 1948 this would have been the Great Western Railway which owned the South Wales ports. After nationalisation of the ports, this duty was carried out by the British Transport Commission (BTC), later restyled British Transport Docks Board. Bucket dredgers (usually not self propelled) working with a number of steam powered hopper barges slowly gave way to diesel-powered grab dredgers in the 1950s and 1960s. The *Kenfig* was one of two similar grab dredgers delivered to the BTC in the mid-1950s by Henry Scarr of Hessle. She was allocated from new in 1954 to Swansea and Port Talbot. She had two diesel-powered grabs and a strange wheelhouse amidships. Mud was discharged via opening hopper doors in the bottom of her hull. The *Kenfig* became outdated after suction dredgers had been introduced. She was transferred to Newport and Cardiff to replace the last bucket dredger in the early 1970s. She was then laid up at Cardiff before being sold in 1983 and renamed *Hedon Sand*. She was eventually broken up at New Holland in 1989.

A new daily ferry service between Swansea and Cork began in 1969 operated by the British and Irish Steam Packet (B & I Ferries) using a new purpose-built passenger car ferry the *Innisfallen*. She was twin screw and built in Rendsburg. The *Innisfallen* was powered by four 8-cylinder M.A.N. diesels and is seen here arriving Swansea from Cork on 23 June 1971. The route was very popular initially, but by the late 1970s custom had tailed off and she was sold in 1980. Passing to Italian interests as the *Corsica Viva* she went on to have a host of names before ending up with a Turkish owner as the *Derin Deniz* in 2003. She was sold to Indian breakers and arrived at Alang on 14 October 2004. The ferry route between Swansea and Cork has survived and prospered.

The single-screw passenger/cargo vessel *City of Oxford* was a sister ship to the *City of Birmingham* seen on the cover of this book. She was built at John Brown's shipyard on the Clyde but a year earlier in 1948. She had a gross tonnage of 7593 and an overall length of 480 feet. The *City of Oxford* was 23 years old when photographed sailing from Swansea in the setting sun of 17 September 1971. Five years later she was sold for further trading under the Panama flag as the *Union Arabia* and was finally scrapped on the beaches of Taiwan in 1978.

The *Sangaetano* was a Liberty ship built way back in 1944 as the *Samtrusty*. She was completed by the Bethlehem-Fairfield Shipyard at Bethlehem, near Baltimore, and had triple expansion machinery. Seen here arriving unladen on the morning tide of 4 September 1969, the *Sangaetano* was by now under the Liberian flag and operated by Cia. de Nav. "Somerset", of Lugano, Switzerland. Careful study of surfaces near deck level will reveal a brown dust, which may indicate that she has not long ago discharged a cargo of ore. Otherwise she is in fine condition despite her dated design.

Swansea was the last South Wales port to continue exporting coal from the South Wales coalfield. A number of coal hoists survived well into the 1980s. Vessels of many nationalities bound for ports throughout Europe would load coal beneath these hoists. The *Corburn* was a British motor collier belonging to Cory Maritime Limited of London. She was built by the Goole Shipbuilding and Repairing Co Ltd in 1953. This study of her in October 1970 will reveal that a coal wagon is actually being discharged into the vessel. *Corburn* continued to sail for Cory until 1972 when she became the *Aigeorgis* changing to *Georgis* in 1976, both under the Greek flag. She was laid up at Piraeus in July 1978 and sold to Italian breakers at Brindisi in September 1979.

Ships of Ellerman's Wilson Line never traded to ports in the Bristol Channel. It was therefore very unusual to see the green-hulled *Rapallo* in Swansea. She was however laid up for a period in the Prince of Wales Dock during 1971 and seen here on 3 May. Being only 11 years old, needless to say she went back into service. Built as a refrigerated cargo vessel by the Henry Robb shipyard at Leith, the *Rapallo* was powered by a 7-cylinder Clark-Sulzer diesel. An additional feature was that she had two small cargo tanks intended for carrying vegetable oils. In 1972 she was transferred to the associated Ellerman Lines and repainted into their house colours. As such she visited Swansea on at least one occasion and was later renamed *City of Limassol* in 1975. Surplus to requirements, she was sold to Lebanese owners in 1977 for further trading. She was scrapped in Spain in 1986.

The *Lena* was a steamship of 2694 grt, built at Blainville by Ch. Nav. de Caen and dating from 1948, and comes complete with a counter stern. Built as the *Alès*, she became the *Lena* in 1964 under the Liberian flag and operating for Lena Shipping S.A. Here she is seen looking a little worse for wear and laid up in Prince of Wales Dock on 17 February 1970. The Kings Dock was the main cargo handling facility whilst the smaller Prince of Wales Dock was by the 1960s used by trawlers, dredgers, tugs and other service craft.

The elegant *Clan Macdougall* was very much a classic British general cargo ship with a split superstructure arrangement. She was owned by the Houston Line which was part of Clan Line Steamers Ltd. They were involved with trading to the Middle East, India and Ceylon. A thoroughbred Scottish ship, the *Clan Macdougall* was built by the Greenock Dockyard Company, of Greenock, in 1944.

She was a twin-screw motor vessel capable of 16 knots and had some refrigerated cargo space which made her quite versatile. A regular visitor to the Bristol Channel even in the late 1960s, she is seen making her way towards the lock on 1 June 1970. Her days were numbered though as she was sold to Taiwan breakers in 1971 and would not return to Swansea again.

Metcalf Motor Coasters painted the hulls and funnels of its ships in a deep green colour and these coasters were quite distinguished in their appearance. All had Metcalf family Christian names followed by the suffix letter M. The *Anthony M* was a small coastal tanker dating from 1944. She was built in Germany as the *Göhren* and came to the UK as part of a reparations payment after the Second World War. At this point she gained the name *Empire Tigity*. In 1953 she received a new Blackstone 480bhp diesel engine. On 24 June 1969 she sets sail from Swansea. Behind is the old western breakwater which would shortly be replaced with a new concrete structure. After leaving the Metcalf fleet she passed to Effluents Services Ltd mainly working out of Goole as *Kinder*. She was eventually sold for demolition at Garston in 1983.

Alexandra Towing of Liverpool took delivery of three attractive steam tugs in 1954. All were products of Cochrane's yard at Selby and the *Wallasey* was the second of the trio, the first being the *Waterloo* and the final one the well-known *Canning*, now preserved in Swansea. They were a compact design and had a useful output of 1000 indicated horse power. The *Wallasey*'s stay on the Mersey was brief as she was transferred to Swansea in 1956 and worked here and at Port Talbot until her sale in 1972. She was sold to a Mr K Radcliffe at Portsmouth and renamed *Kendiken*. She was in permanent lay up on a buoy in Portsmouth Harbour from at least 1977. She moved to a breaker on the River Itchen at Southampton in 1983, and was finally scrapped in 1992. She is photographed here in the Kings Dock towing the tanker *British Merlin* towards the lock on 6 October 1969.

The Corporation of Trinity House employed a small fleet of ships around the UK as buoy and navigation aid/lighthouse tenders. Trinity House had a shore depot at the eastern end of the Kings Dock and a vessel was often to be found moored there. The **Argus** was one of a class of three such vessels built shortly after the war. They were larger than previous ships and had the distinction of being the last steamships built for Trinity House. **Argus** was built in 1948 by Ferguson Bros of Port Glasgow. She was oil-fired and powered by two triple expansion engines driving twin screws. She was withdrawn for scrap in 1974. Here she is leaving Swansea lock on 28 January 1969 with the dredger **Ely** in the background, which was busy dredging the ferry berth on the River Tawe.

Located between Swansea and Port Talbot is the River Neath and Briton Ferry. In the late 1960s the dominant feature was Thomas Ward's ship-breaking wharves. Ship-breaking had taken place at Briton Ferry since the late 1800s and the wharf was known locally as "giants graveyard". The *Pando Sound* arrived from Swansea for breaking up on 11 May 1972. Built in 1954 as *Bendigo*, a general cargo liner for the P & O Steam Navigation Co, of London, she was intended for the UK/Australia general cargo and wool trade. The *Bendigo* was a steam turbine ship constructed in Glasgow by Alexander Stephens and capable of 18 knots. In 1968 she was transferred to the Far Eastern service along with a number of similar ships and renamed *Pando Sound*. Demolition commenced in September 1972, but was still not complete in February 1974 when she broke from her moorings during a storm and became stranded in the middle of the River Neath. She is seen here on 24 August 1972.

A lot of smaller ships ended their days here but the two photographs on this page show that larger vessels too were demolished. The *British Fame* was the first member of the class of twenty vessels referred to on page 5. She was delivered from Swan Hunter's yard at Wallsend in 1949. This class had nine holds, four cargo pumps and a crew of about 48. Some of these ships put in over twenty years service with BP before being sold for scrap. The *British Fame* awaits her fate on 17 February 1972, her masts having been removed so that she could pass under the road bridge. Today there are small but active commercial wharves on the River Neath, including one at Giants Wharf.

These were the twilight years for the original Port Talbot dock. The main trade by the late 1960s was the supply of iron ore to the huge Port Talbot steelworks close by. However a new tidal harbour was constructed and opened in 1970 which could handle very large bulk carriers. This spelt the end though for the old dock which was duly closed, but never filled in. The lengthy approach channel was at the mouth of the River Kenfig to the east of Aberavon beach. The dock system was accessed by a rather small lock with built-in lay-by. The steam tug *Formby* leads the unladen ore carrier *Oremina* away from the lock, while in the background can be seen Aberavon beach and funfair. The *Formby* was built by Cochrane & Sons at Selby in 1951 and was converted from coal to oil burning in 1956. She was sold a few months after this photograph was taken on 12 June 1969. The *Oremina* was one of a class of six similar ore carriers managed by Houlder Bros and on long term charter to the British Iron and Steel Corporation (BISCo). She arrived at Spanish breakers in April 1986.

Stephenson Clarke was a large operator of coastal ships and named most of their vessels after villages in Sussex. Their post-war fleet mainly consisted of motor colliers and included a small fleet of flat-iron colliers designed for working on the Thames. Stephenson Clarke also had a number of coastal tankers. The *Portslade* was a motor collier built in Sunderland in 1955. She had a Clark-Sulzer diesel with an output of 1400bhp. Here she is seen fully laden making her way up the Port Talbot dock system on 9 May 1969. The *Portslade* was sold and became *Sassa* in 1977. She ended her days sailing for Sudanese owners until sold for scrap in March 1985.

After the Second World War there was an increase in demand for steel and the steelworks at Port Talbot was rebuilt with new larger and updated facilities. To coincide with this a new fleet of 24 iron ore carriers of 9500 tonnes deadweight was ordered as a joint venture between the British Iron and Steel Corporation and a number of shipping companies. The main problem facing this new partnership was the restricted lock size at Port Talbot so this new group was designated the "Port Talbot class". The new ore carriers were introduced from the mid-1950s onwards and were operated by a number of mainly British shipping companies. Iron ore was coming from places such as Norway and north and west Africa. Two examples seen here on 23 August 1968 are the *Clarkavon* of 1958 operated by Denholm Ship Management and Houlder Brothers' *Oregis* of 1955.

Two Alexandra Towing tugs were normally kept at Port Talbot and supplemented by the Swansea fleet as required. In the late 1960s these tended to be the *Gower* of 1961 and the older motor tug *Margam* of 1953 which was acquired second-hand in 1966. The *Gower* was the first of a pair of 1200bhp motor tugs built by W J Yarwood at Northwich, the second being named *Talbot*. The *Gower* was launched on 27 March 1961 and was the first tug in the Alexandra fleet with a controllable pitch propeller. When the enclosed dock system at Port Talbot closed, she moved back to Swansea until eventually being sold to Greek owners in 1986 and named *Kostas*. She is seen here sailing close to the iron ore berth at the north end of the docks on 23 August 1968.

The small Turkish general cargo ship *Amasya* is photographed moored on the east side of the main dock. She was built in 1955 at Osaka in Japan and was of 3013 tons gross. She was powered by a 7-cylinder Sulzer oil engine. Her owners, when seen here on 19 August 1969, were noted as D.B Deniz Nakliyati T.A.S. and she was registered in Istanbul.

The drydock at Port Talbot was often host to vessels belonging to the Commissioner for Irish Lights. The *Gannet* of 1954 was one of five similar light vessels ordered from Philip & Son, of Dartmouth, in the early 1950s. They had new features such as electric powered lanterns driven by large diesel generators and the hulls incorporated a bilge keel to reduce rolling in heavy weather. The lanterns are mounted on a steel trelliswork tower forty feet above deck level. The *Gannet* spent most of her life on the Arklow station and is seen in pristine condition on 1 January 1970.

We now move eastwards to Barry. Geest Industries opened a banana import terminal at Barry in the early 1960s and initially used chartered ships. In 1964 the *Geestbay* and *Geestport* were delivered, the first of four new purpose-built ships. They were followed shortly after by the *Geestcape* and *Geesthaven*. The *Geestport* was built in the Netherlands and had a full speed of 21 knots. She was fully refrigerated and could carry 12 passengers to and from the Windward Islands in the Caribbean. The evening sun of 28 August 1968 greets her arrival at her UK destination. These ships were easily recognisable by their immaculate white colour scheme and twin funnels mounted at high level. A further four similar vessels were delivered in 1972/73, and the *Geestport* was sold to Afromar Inc. of Greece. She was renamed *Kimlos* and scrapped in 1985.

From time to time the observer could be rewarded with a real "golden oldie" at any of the South Wales ports. On 8 August 1971 the Panamanian flag steam cargo vessel *August* of 1652 gross tons arrives at Barry with pit props for use in the South Wales coalfield. As can be seen, no deck space has been wasted. This veteran of 1935 was built at Burntisland in Fife as the *Thelma*. When photographed, she was owned by Cia. Maritima Dover S.A., based in Hull despite the title, and would have sailed from one of the Baltic ports with her cargo. Ships could enter Barry through the normal lock or through the tidal basin which was also known as No. 3 Dock.

(Bob Allen)

The town of Barry had two large chemical plants producing plastics. These were served by the occasional specialised tanker visiting the port's No. 2 dock. On this occasion, 15 July 1972, we see the liquefied gas carrier *Hoegh Scout* discharging. She was owned by A/S Alliance, a company managed by Leif Hoegh & Co, and she flew the Norwegian flag. She was launched at Kristiansand, Norway, in 1968 as *Rita* but completed as *Hoegh Scout*. Of note is her rather small funnel.

The port of Barry had a licence to handle military explosives cargoes. These were destined for, amongst other places, the Ministry of Defence underground stores at Caerwent near Chepstow, and came from the United States. For safety reasons, a fully laden vessel was not permitted to enter the dock and so the ammunition was discharged at designated anchorages off the port using a small fleet of barges and coasters. The US Navy vessel *Wyandot* was typical of the type of ship used to bring this dangerous cargo from the United States. She was built at Oakland, California, in 1944 as *AKA92*. She was an "Andromeda" class Attack Cargo Ship. The *Wyandot* was steam turbine propulsion, and had a service speed of around 16.5 knots. Seen unladen in No. 1 Dock about to sail in May 1969, she would later go into long-term lay up in March 1976 at Suisun Bay, near Benecia in California.

In my opinion the Cardiff and Barry tugs always looked smarter in the colours of R & J H Rea Ltd compared to those of Cory Ship Towage which were applied later. At the time of this photograph taken on 13 October 1968, Barry was home to three tugs. These were the *Plumgarth* of 1960, and the two identical sisters *Bargarth* and *Uskgarth* of 1966. Cardiff had four tugs one of which was a spare tug. The *Bargarth* was the fourth of a series of four more-or-less identical vessels delivered in 1966. These new tugs displaced the last of the steam tugs. *Bargarth* was launched in April 1966 by Richards Shipbuilders at Lowestoft and had a Blackstone engine driving a fixed pitch propeller in a steerable Kort nozzle. Unlike her three sister tugs, *Bargarth* was fitted with a radar from new which is clearly visible in this view. She remained a Cardiff and Barry tug for 35 years until she was sold in 2002 when she passed to Bilberry Shipping at Waterford in Ireland without a change of name.

Vessels of the Irish Lights fleet used the drydock at Barry as well as that at Port Talbot. On a very sunny 13 October 1968 we see a lightship from the South Rock light station (most probably the *Osprey*) receiving attention. Behind her is the Irish Lights tender *Atlanta* which would have brought the lightvessel to Barry. She was built in 1959 by Philip & Son at Dartmouth and was twin-screw with diesel-electric propulsion. She had bridge control of her engines and a top speed of 13 knots. The *Atlanta* served the Commissioners of Irish Lights for an impressive 29 years and was not broken up until 1991.

The import of pumice stone would bring the occasional dry bulk carrier to Barry's No. 2 Dock. It is 14 February 1971, the day before the introduction of decimal currency in the UK. I doubt whether this would have had much impact on the *Cheviot* or her crew as she waits to discharge her cargo. The *Cheviot* was built in Sunderland, and was the last of four similar ore carriers for the Bamburgh Shipping Co Ltd to be delivered between 1958 and 1961. Bamburgh Shipping was a subsidiary of W A Souter & Company of Newcastle upon Tyne, and the four ships were named after places of historic interest in Northumberland. The *Cheviot* made regular appearances at Cardiff and Newport with iron ore, but was sold in 1977. She passed to the Trico Corporation of Greece and was renamed *Dapo Trader* until being laid up in 1982. Two years later she was renamed *Trader* for her final voyage to the breakers at Setubal in Spain.

In the early 1970s, Barry became a very popular location for British shipping companies to put their ships into short-term lay-up. Both docks were used. Some vessels were sold on whilst others were pressed back into service. The Bristol City Line had been taken over by Bibby Line by the time this shot of the *Halifax City* and *Montreal City* was taken on 3 December 1972. They date from 1964 and 1963 respectively. Both vessels had been laid up in No. 2 Dock and advertised for sale. The state of their orange paintwork suggests that no money was to be spent on them in the run up to their arrival at Barry. Shortly afterwards the pair were sold to buyers in Thailand for further trading. With her new owner, the *Halifax City* caught fire and sank on her first voyage. Her sister continued to sail until scrapped in Thailand in 1986.

The motor ore carrier *Arisaig* was another one of the vessels built specifically to the dimensions of the lock at Port Talbot, namely 427 feet by 57 feet with a maximum draught of 28 feet. This was also a size that made them suitable for the port of Workington in Cumbria. The *Arisaig* was owned by Scottish Ore Carriers Ltd which was a joint venture between Lithgows (the shipbuilder) and the British Iron and Steel Corporation. She was the third of four similar ships with four cargo holds, but the only one to have a diesel engine. She was built on the Clyde in 1957 and scrapped at Faslane in 1972 after only fifteen years trading. She is seen in No. 1 dock with the tugs assisting her on the approach to the nearby drydock on 23 August 1969.

Occasionally it was possible to take advantage of a trip out into Barry Roads on one of the local tugs. This would offer a completely different viewing platform and some pleasantly different photographs could be obtained. In Barry Roads the ore carrier *Ripon* will have already taken on a pilot and is seen picking up tugs before proceeding into Barry. The *Ripon* was one of four similar vessels owned by the North Yorkshire Shipping Co. of Middlesbrough (a joint venture between Bolton Steam Shipping and the British Iron and Steel Corporation). She was scrapped at Santander in 1972.

Our journey eastwards now takes us to Cardiff. By June 1967 when this photograph was taken, the Bute East Dock in Cardiff had ceased to be used for commercial purposes. The two drydocks had fallen into disuse and the dock was used principally for laying up smaller shipping. Vessels of the P & A Campbell fleet as well as dredgers and the redundant Severn crossing ferries could be found tied up awaiting their fate. In amongst these vessels was the Liberian flag steamship *Patrick M* which appeared to have ended her trading days. She was built in 1947 by the Grangemouth Dockyard in Scotland as *Thisbe* and became *Pengly* in 1955 and *Patrick M* in 1966. In the background can be seen the East Moors steel works.

The **Luis Caso de los Cobos** was a very elderly Spanish ship dating from 1919 and operating for Cementos Fradera S.A. She was registered in Aviles and is seen here arriving at Cardiff on 24 April 1968. She was built in Bilbao as the **Chivichiaga**. Unusually for her size, 2493 gross tons, and age she was driven by steam turbines as opposed to a triple expansion engine and indeed was coal-fired. As can be seen she has minimal cargo handling gear. The boat in the foreground was that of the linesman who would be in attendance for most arrivals at Cardiff.

The Shaw, Savill and Albion Line was one of the great shipping companies of the twentieth century. The *Athenic* was a splendid looking refrigerated cargo liner built by Harland & Wolff in 1947 for the Australia and New Zealand trade. Her maiden voyage in August of that year was from London to New Zealand. For this she had accommodation for 85 passengers. Calling at Cardiff in March 1969 on what may well have been her last visit to the UK, she would have brought a cargo of New Zealand lamb together with dairy products such as butter and cheese. Upon discharge, some of this would have been housed in the Empire Cold Stores (the brick building behind the ship) before onward shipment. The *Athenic* was a steam turbine ship and her twin screws could push her through the water at 17 knots. In July 1965 her passenger accommodation was removed. She ended her days later in 1969 driven at full speed onto a beach at Kaohsiung in Taiwan. Here she would have been dismantled to feed the local steel industry.

The motor coaster *Saint Colman* was owned by J & A Gardner & Co Ltd, based in Glasgow, and was built in the Netherlands in 1963. Gardners were quarry owners and at this time were also active in coastal bulk trades such as coal, stone and salt. They were also becoming specialists in heavy lift cargoes such as generators and ships' propellers. The *Saint Colman* is seen looking a little uncared for drifting down the Queen Alexandra dock towards the lock on 2 June 1970. She was sold in 1981 and carried several names before becoming the *St. Colman* in 1999 under the Honduras flag. Her final fate is unknown.

Another elderly Spanish ship visiting Cardiff was the ***Antonio de Satrustegui*** this time dating from 1920. At 3289 gross tons, she was slightly bigger than the ***Luis Caso de los Cobos*** (page 32) and also a more attractive looking ship. She seems to be in original condition with a full set of derricks and was propelled by a triple expansion steam engine. She was built in North Vancouver by Wallace Shipyards Ltd as the ***Canadian Raider***. At 51 years old, she makes a fine sight as she sails from Cardiff on 20 January 1971.

The *Roland* was a regular visitor to Cardiff and often brought in a cargo of crushed animal bones from South America. As the *Roland* she traded for the Lamport and Holt Line, but was in fact built in 1950 as the *Dunedin Star* for Blue Star Line, and sailed as such until 1968. She was a refrigerated steamship of 7344 tons gross built at Glasgow by Alexander Stephens and Sons. The cargo of crushed bones would be sucked out of the ship's hold by special equipment installed on the quay in the Roath Dock. In this view, dated 31 August 1968, we can see this in operation astern of the *Roland*, as bones are unloaded from the *Glenmoor*. After a career of 28 years, the *Roland* was delivered to Pakistani breakers at Gadani Beach in June 1978.

In the early 1950s, Stag Line owned in North Shields by Joseph Robinson, set about a programme of updating its ageing fleet with a series of modern dry-cargo bulk carriers. The *Photinia* of 1961 was the last in a series of four vessels and was completed by J Readhead & Sons Ltd, of South Shields. She was built with a raised quarter deck, five holds and designed for a variety of bulk cargoes such as grain and timber. Stag Line ships were named after flowers and had a distinctive white stag emblem on the funnel. In 1964 the *Photinia* was chartered to British Insulated Callender's Cables (BICC) and adapted for cable laying. She worked as such in New Zealand and Canada, but resumed her traditional role after these contracts ended. She is seen here discharging grain at the Spillers berth on 18 May 1968. The grain silo is in the background. She was chartered to BICC once again in 1976 for further cable laying in the Cook Strait, New Zealand. Whilst waiting for a berth at Milwaukee in May 1978, she was driven aground after dragging her anchors. She was declared a constructive total loss.

A sand wharf was established in the "cut" between the Roath Basin and the Bute East Dock after the latter was officially closed. Bowles (later British Dredging) used this berth continuously for a good number of years. On 20 August 1968, the steam sand dredger *Camerton* discharges her cargo, much of which would be destined for the local building trade. The *Camerton* was built in 1950 by the Ailsa Shipbuilding Company, of Troon. She was the last steam dredger in the Bristol Channel when sold in 1973. She went for further service in Greece as the *Archonto* but her final fate is unknown.

Tankers of the Onassis Group would from time to time call at Cardiff. The Liberian flag *Olympic Rainbow* of 1954 was a very good example of a steam turbine tanker. She was built in Bremen and was owned for most of her life by Maryland Ltd S.A. She is seen here in January 1971 making some dense black smoke at the oil berth in Cardiff's Queen Alexandra dock. She was sold in 1972 to other Liberian-flag operators and renamed *Hesnes Erik*. In 1973 she sustained boiler damage and was sold to shipbreakers in Taiwan.

The Moss Hutchison Line only operated seven ships when the **Kantara** was photographed sailing from Cardiff on 27 May 1971. They were all of a similar size and design with four cargo holds. The company was taken over by P & O as long ago as 1935, but retained its separate identity until the 1970s. The main trade route was from the UK to various Mediterranean destinations such as Malta, Cyprus and Egypt. The **Kantara** dated from 1947 when she was built by Harland and Wolff at Belfast. She could best be described as a small general cargo vessel of the open shelter deck type. She had some refrigerated capacity. She was sold to Adami Shipping, Cyprus in 1972 and eventually renamed **Constantis II**. As such she was broken up at Castellon, Spain, in 1980.

The tug fleet at Cardiff and Barry was continuously changing in the years 1960 to 1966. Owners of the existing tug fleets were replacing older steam tugs with newer but still outdated examples. Then in late 1961 competition came in the shape of R & J H Rea Ltd, who moved 4 tugs across from Avonmouth. The Dutch-built **Tregarth** was one of these. Shortly after, Rea took over the existing fleets and four new vessels were ordered. These were delivered in 1966 and closely followed the design of the earlier **Lowgarth** which was delivered in 1965. After the arrival of these new tugs, the **Tregarth** became the spare tug at Cardiff.

She was built in 1958 as the **Neylandia** for Milford Haven Services (Overseas Towage and Salvage). She passed to Rea in October 1961 along with sister tug **Cleddia** which became **Falgarth**. She had a German Deutz engine of 500bhp and was also fitted with a Kort nozzle. Clearly of Dutch design, she was a fascinating little tug and had a very distinctive exhaust note. The **Tregarth** was sold by Rea in 1970 shortly before the Rea business passed to Cory Ship Towage. The **Tregarth** was purchased by Wimpey Marine and sent to work in Trinidad. Some reports indicate that she later sank whilst working from Trinidad.

The **Portsmouth** was another of Stephenson Clarke's self-trimming colliers that traded around the UK coast. She was built by J Crown at Sunderland in 1950 and had an 8-cylinder Sulzer diesel of 1125bhp. Incidentally she was the first ship to be fitted with this type of engine. The **Portsmouth** had four holds and was capable of 11 knots. Her master and two officers were accommodated in the bridge structure, but all other officers and crew were to be found aft. She was sold in 1971 to Cypriot buyers, Lygia Shipping Co, and became **Sanadreas**. She is seen here as such in the Roath Basin on 5 June 1973. Her old name is still just about visible on the bow.

1968 was the first season that P & A Campbell operated without any paddle steamers. They had to charter a vessel during 1968 and 1969 to cover their summer timetable activities and the modern passenger cargo vessel **Queen of the Isles** was brought in from the Isles of Scilly Steamship Company. She was built by Charles Hill at Bristol in 1965 as a relief ship for the Penzance to St Marys service, but was never really required. She was a twin screw vessel capable of 13 knots and was put to work for Campbells mainly on the South Coast. She is seen here at the Pier Head on 3 April 1969. Upon return to her owner in 1970 she was deemed surplus to requirements and put up for sale. She was sold to the Tonga Shipping Agency for £150,000 and renamed **Olovaha**. She was put to work on the Tongan inter-island service with occasional voyages to Suva and Fiji. She stranded in 1977 and may not have been salvaged

The *Finnamore Meadow* was one of the regular ore carriers to visit Cardiff. She was built by Austin & Pickersgill at Sunderland in 1961 for Falaise Ore Carriers Ltd, and registered in London. This company was managed by Mavroleon Bros, the well known London-Greek shipping company and ship managers. She is seen here on 4 February 1973 as she discharges at the iron ore berth with East Moors steel works and its fumes in the background. In 1977 she passed to Seas Carriers Corporation of Liberia. She was renamed *Don Manuel*, but remained under the management of Mavroleon Bros. She suffered a serious engine room fire whilst under repair at Naples in 1978, but was repaired and continued to trade. She was named *Palmidi* when eventually scrapped at Vigo in April 1982.

3 November 1972 was not a good day for one of the Cardiff pilots, but neither will it go down in history as a good day for the Reardon Smith Line. Their bulk carrier *New Westminster City* was less than twelve months old at the time of this incident just off Penarth Head. Having travelled half way around the world from British Columbia on the Pacific coast of North America, the Cardiff-owned ship has failed to make the last half mile into the Queens lock. She was refloated on the next high tide and towed into port to discharge her cargo. Such was the damage to her hull that repairs took two months to complete. The *New Westminster City* was one of seven similar bulk carriers built by Upper Clyde Shipbuilders at Govan for Reardon Smith in the early 1970s. The design was termed the "Cardiff" class by her builders who went on to build several similar vessels for other customers. At 16704 gross tons and with five deck cranes she was ideal for transporting large quantities of timber. Having been sold by Reardon Smith, she continued to trade until scrapping took place at Alang, India, in 1998.

The **Amastra** was a member of Shell's "A" class of intermediate size tankers that followed on from the slightly earlier "H" and "K" classes. Most of the class were steam turbine powered, and all but two (**Aluco** and **Arianta**) were of a similar design with bridge and accommodation located amidships. They traded worldwide and were regular visitors to the Bristol Channel for drydocking and repairs. The **Amastra** dated from 1958 and was built at the Smith's Dock shipyard in Middlesbrough. Completed for Tanker Finance Ltd, of London, (part of the Shell group), she was one of the motor variants and had a 6-cylinder Doxford engine that pushed her along at 14.5 knots. She is seen here arriving at Cardiff for a much needed drydocking and repaint on 22 July 1971. Most of the "A" class were disposed of in the 1980s and the **Amastra** was broken up at Chittagong in April 1985.

Between the Rivers Taff and Ely, Esso had a large tank farm on a spur of land which was served by road, rail and sea. Small tankers would berth at a wooden jetty located on the River Ely which was of course tidal. The *Esso Lyndhurst* is seen proceeding towards this berth on 29 August 1970. The Esso Petroleum Company operated fleets of both ocean going and coastal tankers under the British flag. The *Esso Lyndhurst*, 856 tons gross, was an attractive coastal motor tanker of 1958. She was built by Henry Scarr, of Hessle. She would have regularly been used for providing fuel oil bunkers to larger ships. She was sold to Saudi Bunkering Transport Co. in 1980 and renamed *Bunker 1*. She was probably scrapped in the late 1980s.

Now nearing the end of our journey along the Welsh coast, we come to Newport. Ships of the Blue Funnel Line were not that particularly common at Newport and so the appearance of the *Talthybius* was of particular note. She was a standard Victory ship built in 1944 as the *Salina Victory*. She was sold to the Ocean Group in 1946 and became the *Polydorus* under the Dutch flag. She was then transferred to Blue Funnel Line in 1960 and renamed *Talthybius*. In her final year she operated in the colours of the Elder Dempster Line before being sold to Taiwanese breakers in 1971. She is being turned in Newport's South Dock by the dock tug *Newport* on 28 September 1968.

Left: We have already seen examples of two sizes of ore carrier built for long term charter to the British Iron and Steel Corporation. The total number of vessels involved came to 73 of which five were classed as the "larger" type with a deadweight of 25,000 tonnes or more. One of these was the *Gothland* which was built in 1961 for the Leith company Currie Line Ltd. She was built by Lithgows at Port Glasgow who had built several ore carriers by this time. She is seen in the main entrance lock at Newport in September 1967 waiting to be collected by the dock tugs and taken to her berth. The entrance lock at Newport was the largest in the Bristol Channel at the time, being 1000 feet long by 100 feet wide. This compared to Cardiff which was only 850 feet by 90 feet. The extra ten feet width at Newport enabled the tugs to be able to squeeze alongside most regular size ships. Sold in 1977, she was renamed *Dapo Sky*. On 22 August 1978 whilst outbound from Glasgow, she suffered an accommodation fire in the River Clyde. Deemed uneconomic to repair, she was sold to breakers at Faslane the following year.

Below: In addition to the 24 Port Talbot size ore-carriers built for charter to the BISCo, there were 44 larger ships of around 15000 tonnes deadweight, and approximately 505 to 525 feet in length and 69 feet beam. Most were built in British shipyards. The St. Andrews Shipping Company was a joint venture between Denholm (51%) and BISCo (49%) and operated four similar ore carriers. One of these was the *Duncraig* seen here discharging her cargo at the Middle Quay iron ore berth on 7 July 1970. Visible is a plume of steam from one of her auxiliary boilers. The *Duncraig* was built by Lithgows at Port Glasgow in 1957 and was powered by a 4-cylinder Doxford 2-stroke oil engine of 4500bhp. Along with her sister *Sir Andrew Duncan* she continued her BISCo charter in 1967 under the ownership of the British Steam Shipping Co, of Cardiff, until her sale in 1973. She became the *Mary* under the Greek flag and was eventually scrapped at Gadani Beach in late 1982.

Newport had two iron ore discharge berths and it was often possible for both to be in use and to see at least one fully laden vessel waiting for a berth. The *Rievaulx* is doing just that at the west end of the South Dock in June 1968. The steelworks was at Llanwern some distance away and all the ore was moved by rail out of the docks area. When the new tidal harbour opened at Port Talbot, all iron ore imports to Newport ceased and Llanwern received all its iron ore by rail from Port Talbot. Newport docks therefore lost an important source of revenue. The *Rievaulx*, like the *Ripon* on page 30, was one of four similar ships named after towns in North Yorkshire, the other two being the *Redcar* and the *Ribblehead*. The *Rievaulx* was built in 1958 by Smiths Dock of Middlesbrough who also had a small stake in her ownership. After her sale in 1973 to Greek owners, she was involved in a collision at Ushant on the Atlantic Coast of Brittany on 14 June 1974. This incident resulted in the sinking of the cargo vessel *Natcrest* (formerly the British *Riseley* of 1957). Ten years later she was scrapped in China.

47

Towage at Newport was quite interesting as it involved two fleets working together. The British Transport Docks Board had three tugs which were referred to as "dock" tugs. These would handle all movements from the lock to the berth and vice versa. Arrivals and sailings from the lock were the responsibility of Newport Screw Towing. This arrangement came to an end in April 1977. The dock tug *Llanwern* was a sturdy looking twin-screw vessel built in 1960 by P K Harris & Sons Ltd. of Appledore in Devon. Her hull followed the hydroconic design that was popular in the late 1950s and 1960s, and she was also fitted for firefighting. The *Llanwern* was one of a pair but differed from her sistership *St Woolas* as she had diesel-electric propulsion. This resulted in some interesting whining sounds from her electric motors whilst manoeuvring. She is seen picking up her next tow in the lock on 18 April 1970. The *Llanwern* went on to work at Londonderry as *Foyledale* for many years. She later became *Ullapull* working around the UK coast and in 2000 went to work in West Africa as the *Luba*.

The **Dunosprey** is seen approaching the lock at Newport in April 1970 having sailed a ship. In 1968 Newport Screw Towing replaced their last two steam tugs, **Dunhawk** and **Dunfalcon**, with two motor vessels. The **Dunheron** was purchased second-hand but the **Dunosprey** was a new build. She closely followed the specification of the two earlier motor tugs **Duncurlew** and **Dunsnipe** of 1962. She was built on Humberside by R Dunston (Hessle) Ltd and had a 6-cylinder British Polar 2-stroke diesel of 1260bhp. Her wheelhouse was of an improved design and she had bridge control of her main engine. She did not however have a gearbox which allowed ahead and astern operation. To go astern, her engine would have to be stopped and reversed - quite primitive for 1968. The **Dunosprey** passed to Cory Ship Towage in 1971 with the Newport Screw Towage business, and within a short time was transferred to the Belfast fleet. She transferred back to South Wales briefly in 1992, but local tug crews found her unsuitable for work in the area at the time. After a spell on the Medway as **Linda Bennett**, she became an unpowered house boat at Strood Marina.

The *Pegu* was new in 1961 to the Henderson Line of Glasgow for their service to Burma. She was an open shelter deck type general cargo ship of 5764 tons gross. She had five holds of which No. 3 was a deep tank and could be used for vegetable oil. Henderson Line had been acquired by Elder Dempster Lines in 1952 but was kept as a separate operation for the Burma services. This came to an end in 1967 when the Suez Canal was closed due to hostilities. Henderson Line was then disbanded. However the *Pegu* had already been transferred to Elder Dempster in 1966 for use on their West African routes, and then appeared in the colours of the subsidiary Guinea Gulf Line in the same year. She is seen departing Newport in Guinea Gulf colours one sunny Saturday afternoon in September 1968. Of note is the use of a pink colour boot topping and her grey masts and derricks. She was back with Elder Dempster in 1972 and sailing for Guinea Gulf Line again in 1975. Surprisingly she was not sold until 1980 when she passed to a company registered in the Isle of Man and curiously renamed *Regu*. She was scrapped in Taiwan in 1983.

The *Devon* was built for the Federal Steam Navigation Company in 1946 by A Stephen & Sons Ltd, of Glasgow. When built, she was a practical but not very elegant looking ship. The *Devon* was a steam turbine refrigerated cargo ship with five holds, and capable of 16 knots. She was nearing the end of her career when seen here on the repair berth at Newport on 21 June 1969. She was too large for the drydock at Newport so would have only been receiving some floating repairs including some new paintwork on her hull areas. She was scrapped at Hong Kong in July 1971.

Newport was certainly not renowned as a major shipbuilding port in the twentieth century. However there was a shipyard at the mouth of the River Usk which built a handful of small vessels until the late 1960s. The *Nkwanta* was one of a series of six stern trawlers built for the Ghana Fishing Corporation. She was completed in 1969, and like most members of this class, her delivery was delayed as her owners were unable to complete payment at the appropriate time. The trawlers were laid up at Newport pending settlement upon which they were delivered. She is seen here on 18 April 1970 returning to the lock after a trial. She was still fishing in 2006 as the *Afko 203*.

Arriving on the afternoon tide of 29 March 1969 was this former Liberty ship, the *Ispahan*. Her starboard anchor is out of its hawse pipe indicating that she may well have been waiting in Barry Roads prior to making her way up to Newport. She is fully laden and the sky over the Bristol Channel looks threatening. By now flying the Maltese flag, the *Ispahan* was built as the **David Hewes** becoming the **Punta Alice** in 1947 and finally *Ispahan* in 1964. She was a mass produced ship from the Permanente Metals Corporation (Shipyard No. 2) at Richmond, California, in 1943 and had a gross tonnage of 7156 tons.

The refrigerated cargo ship *Hertford* is seen here loading general cargo at the South Quay on 11 May 1973. She was one of a class of eight similar open shelter deck ships built for the Federal Steam Navigation Company and the associated New Zealand Shipping Company. She was twin screw and to a six-hold design. She was delivered in 1948 by Vickers-Armstrong Ltd at Newcastle and had two 5-cylinder Doxford engines which gave her a speed of 16 knots. In 1973 all ships operating for companies in the P & O Group were absorbed into the P & O General Cargo Division and received new corporate funnel colours as seen in this view. The blue funnel colour does not really suit her. The *Hertford* was sold for further trading in 1976 as *Thia Despina* under the Cypriot flag. She was the only one of her class to see further service, but this did not last long as she ran aground near Suez in 1977. She was declared a constructive total loss and towed to Aliaga for demolition.

The latter half of the 1960s heralded a new era in shipping. Containerisation was getting underway and a host of new services from the UK around the world were being established. A new short sea container service started in the late 1960s between Newport and Southern Ireland. For this venture a small German coaster, the *Rolf*, was chartered by B & I Line from her owner Otto Becker, of Hamburg. She was a modern vessel being built in 1967 by the J J Sietas shipyard on the outskirts of Hamburg and is an example of the yard's Type 33d standard design. Of the six ships in this group, she was the only one to have no cargo gear and was perhaps built with container cargoes in mind. The large goalpost mast in front of her superstructure looks a little out of place. The *Rolf* was powered by an Atlas-Mak diesel at up to 12 knots. Here she is inbound at Newport with a slight list to starboard on 31 May 1969.

To complete our survey, we move to the English side of the Bristol Channel. The *Pizzaro* was a fine looking steam turbine cargo vessel of the Pacific Steam Navigation Co. She was built in 1955 by the Greenock Dockyard Company for the west coast of South America service. The *Pizzaro* was one of five similar vessels, four of which came from the Greenock shipyard. Later in her life she would trade to Bermuda and Caribbean ports as well. She was registered in Liverpool and was powered by Parsons Marine Turbines which gave her a speed of 16 knots. She is seen here arriving at Avonmouth on 1 September 1972. Shortly after this P. S. N. sold her to Greek owners who named her *Kavo Maleas*. She was broken up in Taiwan in 1974.

On 14 April 1972, the **Port Albany** was an unusual visitor to Avonmouth. She was one of a class of three similar ships built for service between Australia and Japan and was not to be seen in British waters early on in her life. She was a refrigerated cargo ship with tween deck tanks aft that could be used to carry vegetable oils or molasses. The **Port Albany** was delivered to Cunard Line in 1965 from her builders Caledon Shipbuilding & Engineering Co Ltd, Dundee. She was immediately chartered to Port Line and permanently transferred to them in 1968. She was sold later in 1972 to Greek owners and renamed **Marietta**. The **Port Albany** is seen here in the old Avonmouth Dock. The Avonmouth port complex comprised two main docks. The smallest, Avonmouth Dock, was completed in 1877 followed by the larger Royal Edward Dock in 1908. There was also an oil dock that could be closed off with a floating boom.

With her very distinctive orange coloured hull, the *Toronto City* is seen arriving at Avonmouth on 28 March 1969. She was one of the last pair of ships delivered to the Bristol City Line in 1966. The Bristol City Line operated from Avonmouth to Canada and the Great Lakes calling at other Bristol Channel ports en route. The *Toronto City* and her sister *Coventry City* were built at Sunderland to quite a high specification. They were ice strengthened refrigerated ships capable of 17 knots and fitted with a controllable pitch propeller. They could also accommodate four passengers. Unlike the two earlier ships (see page 32), this pair had cranes as well as derricks. Bristol City Line became part of Bibby Line in 1971. She was eventually broken up in India in 1985.

One of the best known Liverpool-based shipping companies was the Brocklebank Line. By the 1960s, the Brocklebank Line was serving the Middle East, India, Pakistan as well as being involved in worldwide tramping. The *Mathura* was built in 1960 by the Scottish shipbuilder Wm Hamilton & Co Ltd, of Port Glasgow. She was a steam turbine ship of 8782 tons gross and measured 497 feet in length by 63 feet in beam. She had bipod masts and featured a 70 ton derrick. Brocklebank ships were quite rare visitors to the Bristol Channel and so it was a surprise to see the *Mathura* in the Royal Edward dock on 19 May 1968. She was sold in 1972 to Greek owners and renamed *Eurytion*. By 1976 she had become the *Alwaha* and was reported to be on fire at Aden in September 1977. Her next voyage would be to shipbreakers in Pakistan.

The South African Marine Corporation Ltd operated four similar single-screw steam turbine general cargo ships that were all new in the early 1950s. The *S. A. Trader* was built as the *Sjoa* by Fairfield Shipbuilding & Engineering Co Ltd at Glasgow in 1954 for Global Marine Transport under the Panamanian flag. She passed to South African Marine in 1958, and gained the name *South African Trader*, changing to *S. A. Trader* in 1966. She was registered in Cape Town and had a speed of 15 knots. Her owners traded mainly between Europe and South Africa. She is in the Royal Edward Dock discharging on 26 January 1969. In May 1972 she suffered an engine room explosion and fire en route from Mozambique to Italy. She was badly damaged and was sold for scrap shortly after this.

During the Second World War the United States built large numbers of standard design ships in its yards. These included Liberty ships and Victory ships. A standard tanker design was the T2 which was produced in quite large numbers. Many were heavily rebuilt and put in many years service. There were believed to be some still sailing in the 1990s. The **Esso Glasgow** was built in 1942 by the Sun Shipbuilding & Drydock Co in Chester, Philadelphia, as **Wauhatchie**. She had a steam turbine driving electric propulsion with an output of 6000shp. In 1947 she became the **Esso Glasgow** and remained in original condition for ten years. In

August 1957, she was fitted with a new midship section by Harland & Wolff to enable her to carry different grades of fuel. Time has just about run out for her here as she arrives at Avonmouth on 4 June 1971 despite her pristine condition. A month later she arrived at Bilbao in northern Spain for breaking up. This was a sad end to a classic tanker that retained her original funnel to the end. In reality she was lucky to last this long, as in December 1959 when fully laden with aviation fuel, she was involved in a collision on the Houston Ship Canal in thick fog but she survived.

In the 1960s there were two tug operators who undertook ship handling duties at Avonmouth. The *Sea Alert* was the first large motor tug for the C J King fleet. She was delivered in 1960 from Henry Scarr's yard at Hessle whose builders plate is clearly visible. She had a 7-cylinder Ruston & Hornsby engine which gave her a bollard pull of just under 10 tonnes. The *Sea Alert* was followed by two similar but slightly more powerful tugs, the *Sea Volunteer* in 1962 and *Sea Merrimac* in 1964. These however came from different yards. She was sold in 1983 to Celtic Diving and Marine of Cork and renamed *Alert*. In 1995 she crossed the Atlantic to Canada and unfortunately sank off the Labrador Coast on 1 November of that year.

Avonmouth was without a doubt the busiest port in the Bristol Channel in the late 1960s and early 1970s. On a good tide, it was possible to witness up to three large ships arriving and one or two sailing, often together with a flotilla of coasters and barges. The Indian flag *Jag Manek* started life as Fearnley & Eger's *Fernleaf* in 1957. She lasted with this owner only until 1963. Seen here on 28 November 1972 she was now owned by the Great Eastern Shipping Company. Alongside her is a floating grain elevator but the barges are not present. Less than a year later she was sold to Panamanian interests and became the *Wan Pao*. After a further change of owner and name she ended up in a damaged condition with Taiwanese breakers in June 1977.

The *Apollo* was a smart looking short sea trader built in 1954 for the Bristol Steam Navigation Company. Her sister ship was the *Echo*. Her owners operated a twice weekly Bristol to Dublin service and also a weekly service to Rotterdam and Antwerp. The *Apollo* was built in her home port by C Hill & Sons Ltd and was of 1266 tons gross. She had one large hold and a smaller one forward for refrigerated cargo but was not fitted with any cargo handling gear. She was powered by a British Polar main engine of 1280bhp. In 1968 the *Apollo* and *Echo* were lengthened by 24 feet and the following year adapted to take containers. The *Apollo* is seen building up speed as she leaves the lock at Avonmouth on 30 October 1971. She was laid up at Newport in 1980 before being sold the same year. The *Apollo* still existed in 2005 as the *Paulemose R.* under the flag of St Vincent & the Grenadines but is thought to be laid up.

Right : Avonmouth boasted the largest drydock in the Bristol Channel and could accommodate one average size ship with a smaller vessel for company. The drydock was jointly run by Jeffries and Mountstuart. It witnessed a lot of activity until the 1980s but has sadly been out of use for many years now despite a chronic shortage of active drydock facilities in the UK in the twenty first century. In September 1968, Blue Funnel's *Atreus* of 1951 is seen on the blocks receiving attention. There seems to be some activity around her rudder but no sign of any fresh paint yet. *Atreus* was the sistership of the *Calchas* and was sold to Singapore buyers in 1977. She was scrapped at Taiwan in 1979.

Below : Another spectacular survivor was the Finnish-owned *Atlas*. She started life way back in 1929 as the *Hopedene* for Hopemount Shipping Company, of Newcastle, and became the *Photinia* of Stag Line in 1938. She was converted to oil burning in 1948 and sold to her Finnish owners in 1950. As can be seen she has a counter stern whilst on deck, polythene sheeting is being used to protect her deck cargo, a rather strange arrangement. Not long after this photograph was taken on 21 April 1968, the *Atlas* was sold to Somali owners who managed to obtain another five years out of her. She was eventually scrapped in Yugoslavia in 1974.

As a shipping line Palm Line was a relative newcomer being formed in 1949. It emerged from within the United Africa Company and inherited a motley collection of older ships. They were involved purely in the West African trade and served up to forty ports along 5000 miles of coastline. Their main trade was however with Nigeria and Ghana. In 1954 Palm Line embarked on a programme of fleet modernisation and ordered 14 new motor ships. Twelve of these came from the same yard, Swan, Hunter and Wigham Richardson at Newcastle upon Tyne. The other pair were built in Germany. The *Enugu Palm* and her sister *Elmina Palm*

were a Newcastle-built pair, the *Enugu Palm* being completed in 1958. She is seen here in Avonmouth's Royal Edward Dock in 1973 discharging her cargo which included goods from West Africa. As can be seen in the barges alongside the ship, this included hardwood logs. Some Palm Line ships were designed for "creek work" in Africa. This involved loading from barges in creeks as opposed to being tied up at a wharf. The *Enugu Palm* was sold to Kuwait interests in 1978 and renamed *Athari*. She ended her days being broken up in Karachi in 1982.

The BP tanker fleet took delivery of sixteen products tankers between 1972 and 1974. They were all named after British rivers. This class followed on from two similar designs which included the eleven strong "tree" class delivered in 1964 and 1965. The *British Dart* was a 1972 delivery, one of six built in Gothenburg. She was of 25000 tonnes deadweight, 562 feet in length and designed for world service. She is seen here sailing from Avonmouth on 28 October 1972 when still fairly new. Her BP houseflag can be seen flying above her bridge. The *British Dart* was one of five River class tankers sold to Iranian interests in 1986 and was renamed *Minab 3*. After a career of 32 years, she was sold for scrap arriving at Gadani Beach in April 2004.

The modernisation of R & J H Rea's Avonmouth fleet was completed with the delivery in 1962 of the *Pengarth* and *Polgarth*. They were local products of Charles Hill's shipyard in Bristol. The *Pengarth* was an attractive, handy-sized tug of 160 gross tons. She had a Ruston & Hornsby engine with an output of 1080bhp. Fitted with a controllable pitch propeller, this gave her a bollard pull of 14.5 tonnes.

This view of her was taken on 21 April 1968 between the breakwaters outside the main entrance lock at Avonmouth. When Rea was taken over by Cory Ship Towage in 1971, the *Pengarth* remained at Avonmouth until sold to R J Harvey, of Grimsby, in 1991. Following a spell with Tyne Towage she went to work in Togo, West Africa, as the *Vigilant* for Togo Oil and Marine at the port of Lome.

The *Clan Maclay* was part of Clan Line's post war fleet renewal programme. She was one of a class of six vessels delivered by the Greenock Drydock Company. Four of these were motor vessels, the remaining two were steam turbine. The *Clan Maclay* was a motor example built in 1949 and had a gross tonnage of 6388.

As can be seen from this view of her on 31 March 1973, she has three large pairs of Samson post type derricks. She was sold in 1976 to trade under the Panamanian flag as the *Climax Amethyst* and was broken up in Taiwan in 1979.

The *Cabot* dates from 1952 and was completed as a tug and passenger tender for the Port Authority at Bristol and Avonmouth. She could carry up to 45 passengers if necessary in the saloon beneath her wheelhouse. The *Cabot* was constructed in Bristol by Charles Hill as a twin screw tug of 98 tons and fitted with two small Polar diesels with a combined output of 300bhp. She was re-engined in 1963 and gained a pair of 8-cylinder Gardner engines boosting the output to 400bhp. Her duties included towage and berthing duties for the Port Authority's dredging fleet and she is seen here in charge of the steam bucket-dredger *Evenlode* on 1 September 1971. Other duties could range from assisting with the large floating crane *Bristol Giant* to the more privileged job of transporting civil dignitaries around the port estate at Bristol, Avonmouth or Portishead. She was sold by the Port of Bristol Authority in 1974 to owners on the Thames. After quite an active and varied career she ended her days in the Republic of Ireland being scrapped there in 1995.

The motor hopper barge *King Road* was part of the Port of Bristol Authority's dredging fleet. She was built in 1953 by Lobnitz, of Renfrew on the River Clyde, and had a gross tonnage of 1045. A notice on her accommodation tells us that she is twin screw. She was built to work with the bucket dredger *Evenlode* and would discharge her spoil via opening doors in the bottom of her hull. She is seen heading out to sea from Avonmouth on 26 March 1973. When the use of bucket dredgers was coming to an end, she was renamed *BD15* by her owners, before being sold for use in the Netherlands in 1984. As the *Albatros*, she was scrapped in 1989.

The tanker *Regent Falcon* was on long term charter to Regent Petroleum from ship owner John I Jacobs. She was a regular visitor in the Bristol Channel even after Regent was absorbed into the Texaco empire. She was used for coastal work between refineries and tank farms with refined products such as petrol, diesel and aviation fuel. She is seen here discharging at the oil dock in Avonmouth on 19 May 1968. The *Regent Falcon*, delivered in 1959, was powered by a 6-cylinder opposed-piston Doxford main engine and had two exhaust-gas Scotch boilers. She had 27 oil cargo tanks and 3 steam-driven main cargo pumps. For the officers and crew, she had an open-air swimming pool situated aft. She was built at Haverton Hill on the Tees by the Furness Shipbuilding Company and eventually became the *Texaco Durham* for Texaco in 1972. She was sold in 1975 and eventually scrapped at Gadani Beach in late 1982.

We move up the River Avon to the centre of Bristol. Much of the trade at the Bristol City Docks towards the end of its commercial life was associated with timber and wood products. This included plywood, woodpulp and newsprint as well as softwood such as pine. Much of this came from the Baltic countries and Russian flag ships were very common. The *Lakhta* was a typical Russian cargo vessel which brought in timber to Bristol. She was built in Navashino in 1967 and was of 3167 tons gross. The shipyard was located on the River Oka and some considerable distance from the sea, deep in Russia. She continued trading for many years, latterly as part of the Far Eastern fleet. Under the Belize flag she was scrapped in 2002. On 17 October 1970 she is seen about to discharge her cargo of timber, a large quantity of which has been stowed on deck for the voyage to Bristol. The buildings on the quay now form the Bristol Industrial Museum, which itself is due to close in 2006.

The Royal Fleet Auxiliary ocean-going salvage tug *Cyclone* (Pennant No. A111) was built as the *Growler* in 1943. She was a member of the eight-strong Bustler class which were the first Fleet tugs with diesel engines. The *Cyclone* was built by Henry Robb, of Leith, and had two 8-cylinder Polar diesels of 3020bhp which drove a single propeller and this gave her a bollard pull of 30 tonnes. Periods of charter saw her renamed *Caroline Moller* between 1947 and 1952, *Castle Peak* in 1954, and *Welshman* in 1962. She was an unusual visitor at Bristol on 28 November 1972. The *Cyclone* went on to be based at Gibraltar from 1975 until 1982. After a period in lay up, she was sold by the Ministry of Defence for use at Mombasa and renamed *Martial* under the Cayman Islands flag. She was sold for scrap in 1985.

Bristol City Docks was once a major player in world trade. However being located six miles inland up the River Avon, its restricted access made it unsuitable for larger vessels. In later years trade was mainly confined to coastal vessels serving the UK and Europe. A run-down in activities at the City Docks continued throughout the 1950s and 1960s until the closure of the docks was announced in 1970. The *Arran Firth* was a typical coaster of the 1950s. She was built in 1957 in Holland as the *Alpha* becoming *Arran Firth* in 1962. She was owned by Firth Shipping Co Ltd, (G T Gillie & Blair, managers), of Newcastle upon Tyne. Her gross tonnage was 544 and she is seen alongside the quay at The Grove in the City Docks in January 1969. She was sold in 1970 and the following year passed to Greek owners who renamed her *Agia Markella*. She is thought to have been scrapped in the early 1990s.

(Derek Chaplin)

The end of shipbuilding at the Charles Hill shipyard in Bristol was just around the corner by the late 1960s. Up until about 1964 there had been a steady number of small orders still coming in. Ship repair was a useful sideline and the adjacent drydock was kept busy mainly with local sand dredgers, tugs and coasters. Although not a product of that yard, the tug *Dingle Bay* was quite an unusual visitor in April 1969. She was only about a year old and had major engine problems. She was one of four identical firefighting tugs built for use at the new oil terminal at Bantry Bay in the Republic of Ireland. She was operated by Bantry Bay Towing Company which was a subsidiary of Cory Towage. The *Dingle Bay* was 129 feet long and had a bollard pull of 37 tonnes. The source of the trouble was her 6-cylinder Mirrlees National diesel which had an output of 2520bhp. The terminal at Bantry Bay had closed in 1979 after being damaged in an explosion. She was then sold to Irish Tugs Ltd in 1987 and was by now stationed at Cobh along with her sister the *Tralee Bay*. In 2006 she can be found working at Douala in Cameroon as *Centaure*, still with her Mirrlees KMR-6 engine.

This view of the Cumberland Basin shows Bristol Steam Navigation's *Apollo* and the Norwegian side-loader *Fraternia* waiting to sail. The *Fraternia* is of particular interest. She dates from 1966 and was one of two ships used by Gotha Line on a weekly service bringing timber products from Sweden. She had side doors and was discharged using fork-lift trucks. The *Apollo* had not long been "stretched" when this view was taken on 27 March 1969.

On our way back to the Bristol Channel proper, we pass Pill on the River Avon. Pill has long been associated with Bristol pilots and line handlers in the docks are still known as the "Pill hobblers". The *Hero* and her sister *Dido* were the last ships purchased by the Bristol Steam Navigation Company. They were built to carry steel from South Wales to the Continent but were regular performers on the Dublin to Bristol service. The *Hero* was built in 1963 by Charles Hill at Bristol and had a gross tonnage of 1589. The advent of containerisation meant big changes for many services and the BSNC had to adapt. Despite her age of only seven years, the *Hero* was not considered suitable for permanent conversion to container work and was sold in 1970. Prior to this she did carry a few containers as deck cargo as can be seen in the photograph. She went on to become the *Whitethorn* trading for S William Coe & Co. The *Hero* is seen making her way up the River Avon past Pill in March 1968, most probably inbound from Dublin. The pilot ladder is clearly visible.

(Derek Chaplin)

We are now back on the shore of the Bristol Channel. The small dock at Portishead was opened in 1879 to compete with the newly-opened dock at Avonmouth on the opposite bank of the River Avon. Trade initially focussed on grain and timber imports followed by gasoline. A coal-fired power station was built close to the dock and imports later included coal, phosphates and woodpulp. The Danish motor coaster **Katrine Dancoast** is seen discharging her cargo of woodpulp in July 1971. **Katrine Dancoast** was built in Denmark in 1968 and was owned by Rederlet Dancoast I/S. Albright and Wilson's phosphorus plant saw raw materials arriving in the company's own ships and it was one of these vessels that brought trade to an end at Portishead. The power station closed in 1980 and all commercial activity ceased in 1990. Once a thriving dock, it is now a marina, the fate of too many of our ports.

(Derek Chaplin)

Small tankers would call at Portishead to discharge petrol and diesel for storage and distribution from a nearby tank farm. C J King's small motor tug *John King* is seen towing the fully laden tanker *Esso Fulham* into the dock in August 1967. The *Esso Fulham* was built as the *Trujillo*. She was one of a class of steam tankers built in the United States in 1945 especially for service in Venezuela. When they became surplus to requirements, some were transferred to northern Europe for further use. She had triple expansion machinery and was twin screw. The *John King* on the other hand was built in Bristol in 1936. She was used mainly as a lighterage tug and had a Petter diesel of 300bhp when built. This was replaced in 1962 by a 6-cylinder Lister-Blackstone. She was sold by Kings in 1970 and continued to be based in the Bristol area for a number of years carrying the names *Peter Leigh*, *Pride* and *Durdham*. She is now preserved at the Bristol Industrial Museum as a working exhibit.

(Derek Chaplin)

To conclude, we look at some of the wide variety of smaller vessels to grace the Bristol Channel during the years of our survey. Firstly, we look at two pilot boats. Pilots for Barry, Cardiff, Newport and the Bristol area ports would all join their vessels in Barry Roads. There was a large Pilot Office at the outer harbour in Barry docks, and pilot boats for each port would be moored here. The *Rupert Phillips* was one of the vessels used by Barry pilots and is seen returning to the harbour with the pilot on board. The date is 28 July 1970. In the background are a couple of ships lying in Barry Roads, and in the distance the Somerset hills.

Swansea Bay can be subject to some quite heavy swells and so the pilot vessels serving Swansea and Port Talbot need to be good sea boats. In 1959 the Swansea Pilotage Authority took delivery of a fine new vessel, the *Seamark*. She had two engines but was single screw. Built by P K Harris (Shipbuilders) Ltd, of Appledore, she was 111 feet long by 23 feet in the beam. In 1986 her owners became the Swansea and Port Talbot Pilotage Authority and in 1989 Associated British Ports took control of pilot provision. She is seen here in her attractive yellow, red and white livery leaving Swansea in September 1970. The *Seamark* lasted at Swansea until 2001 when she was moved to Cardiff and donated to the Cardiff Sea Cadet Corps the following year.

We now see two training vessels. The **Margherita** was operated by the Nautical College at Llandaff in Cardiff for over twenty five years. She was built for the Ministry of Defence as one of the "HAM" class inshore minesweepers constructed between 1952 and 1957. All had wooden hulls and a pair of Paxman diesel engines each driving a propeller. She was initially based at Barry but later used Cardiff's Roath Basin as her base. In the 1980s she was rebuilt with a new enlarged wheelhouse and continued her role as a training vessel for Merchant Navy cadets and officers. She was a fast vessel but not a particularly good sea boat, and had a tendency to roll violently in rough conditions. Here she is seen in her original condition in July 1970 just entering the lock at Barry. Upon closure of the Nautical College in Cardiff, it is believed that she was sold to Vosper Thorneycroft in the early 1990s for use as a private yacht based at Gosport.

The Sail Training Association commissioned two purpose built sailing vessels in the 1960s. They were both three-masted steel hull schooners. The first the **Winston Churchill** was delivered in 1966. She was followed by the Aberdeen-built **Malcolm Miller** in 1968. Their purpose was to provide a training facility for young people by undertaking cruises around the UK and northern Europe. The **Malcolm Miller** could accommodate a 55-strong crew. Many of these would be young people. She visited Cardiff on a number of occasions and was one of the last ships to use the Bute East Basin in June 1969 before it was filled in. She is decorated with a full set of bunting to mark the occasion of her visit. The **Malcolm Miller** paid off on 5 December 1999 at Weymouth and was sold the following year. She can now be found sailing in the Caribbean as the privately-owned **Helena C**.

We conclude our survey at Ilfracombe with a reminder of the pleasure to be had by sailing on the Bristol Channel. The **Westward Ho** previously sailed as **Vecta** in the Red Funnel fleet at Southampton. Here she had been in use as a passenger and car ferry on the Southampton to Cowes service and had capacity for 20 average size cars. In 1965 she was purchased by Townsend Car Ferries and put to work in the P & A Campbell fleet. When built in 1938, she was quite revolutionary in that she had a pair of Voith-Schneider propulsion units. However, frequent blade damage meant that in 1946 she was converted to conventional twin-screw propulsion. Before entering service with P & A Campbell she had her car deck converted into a passenger saloon which increased her gross tonnage from 630 to 739 tons. The **Westward Ho** was employed mainly in the upper Bristol Channel until 1971 when her engines started giving trouble. She was laid up at Barry and sold for use as a static restaurant in Manchester. She was eventually broken up on the River Thames. Here we see her arriving at Ilfracombe in pleasant evening light on 24 July 1971. This was to be her last season.

(Nigel Jones)